M000031105

MAKE HIM
FALL FOR YOU

RORI RAYE

BY RORI RAYE

Have The Relationship You Want

Heart Connection Toolkit

Reconnect Your Relationship

Commitment Blueprint

Toxic Men

The Modern Siren

Targeting Mr. Right

MAKE HIM
FALL FOR YOU

RORI RAYE

Have The Relationship You Want, LLC

MAKE HIM FALL FOR YOU

Copyright 2010 by Have The Relationship You Want, LLC

For information:

Rori Raye

http://www.HaveTheRelationshipYouWant.com

ISBN **978-0-578-05838-2**

Any reproduction, republication or other distribution of this work, including, without limitation, the duplication, copying, scanning, uploading and making available via the Internet of any other means, without the express permission of the publisher is illegal and punishable by law, and the knowing acquisition of an unauthorized reproduction of this work may subject acquirer to liability. Please purchase only authorized electronic or print editions of this work and do not participate in or encourage electronic piracy of copyrighted materials. Your support of the author's rights is appreciated.

To you...
a woman who's struggled so valiantly with
what we've all been taught are the "true rules"
about men, love and romance, and then
painfully discovered (as I did) that those rules
are not, and have never been – true, these tools
are dedicated. I feel honored to accompany you
on your road to your Happy Ever After.

I know that you can brush past all those rules
and lies, and that your dreams of romance and
love, and all you want and deserve – will
quickly find you.

TABLE OF CONTENTS

A Note From Me To You

Long, long ago, I thought I was doomed to failure in love. I thought I'd bit the dust, exhausted everything I knew how to do to get love, disappointed my mother and my friends, and humiliated myself before every man I'd ever loved and lost.

And then I woke up.

I suddenly realized what was going wrong. I suddenly got why men seemed so great – but just not for me.

At least not for me past a date or two. Definitely not past sex. (Except, of course, for the men I didn't really like – the ones my mother would have approved of...the ones I thought I was supposed to end up with...the ones I couldn't square with what I felt – and then, too, the ones who stuck around – unbeknownst to me – as "friends with benefits.")

I came face-to-face with my enemy. And it wasn't men or fate, or prettier women.

It was the voice in my head that told me lies about men and fate and prettier women.

It was the voice in my head that told me I wasn't enough. That I had to DO something to get love, and I'd better figure out what that was quick, or I was going to end up alone forever.

Well, it wasn't what I figured out to DO that turned my love life around, it was what I learned, finally, NOT to do.

The big word for me was "pretend."

And, if you asked me, I couldn't even pick out what it was that I was pretending – because it was ALL pretend.

I was even pretending with myself, when I was alone. The words I spoke into my own ear were the same lies I was hearing in my head…and I finally heard them for what they were – "pretending not to be afraid."

The moment I got that it was okay to be afraid, everything turned around for me. Then I got that it was okay to be angry, and that made things even better. Then I got that I actually could "choose" a man – not just get swept along after my chemical whims.

When I finally got that I was enough, without *doing* anything, I met the man who would be my husband…and from there, the story just begins.

These Tools work.

They work because they are not about pretending – but because they are the opposite. They will help you tear down that wall of pretend between yourself and a man so that a good man can finally see you.

See who you are, how you are…and experience what it's like to actually be with *you* – not the pretend you.

To do this…it takes baby-steps – because the path to our real selves is the one we've tried to *avoid* all our lives. We don't really want to go there.

So – these Tools provide immediate rewards – to encourage you to stay on the path to your Happy Ever After:

As you do a Tool, there'll be something new for you – a new way to see, a new way to be, a new way to receive the love you deserve instead of going after it in a way that will never, ever work. And you'll see a result with a man almost immediately.

If you're already receiving my free newsletters, these Tools may not be new for you – they are versions of Relationship Tools of the Week you may have seen or will see. I was asked so many times to put my favorites into a collection for the bookshelf and for gifts…and so here it is.

To get my newsletters, like these, free to your email, go to:

www.HaveTheRelationshipYouWant.com, or

interact with me on my blog community at:

http://blog.HaveTheRelationshipYouWant.com.

Be sure to let me know how the Tools work for you…I love hearing from you and look forward to helping you any way I can.

Love, Rori

1

Be His Pearl

Have you ever felt like a man is a "stranger"?

Like he has no idea who you *are*, and even worse — he doesn't CARE?

I remember feeling like every man I loved thought I was "expendable." Like I was there for his "convenience" — I was "disposable."

I was *always* a Stepping Stone for another woman, I was always a "transition" woman, I always felt like I was in a never-ending DEAD-END.

Like the Dead-End would just go on forever. I couldn't see the end, I just knew it was dead.

And meanwhile, other women would be cozying up to wonderful men, settling into homes and relationships and marriages and children, moving on with their lives and their dreams, and just, well...becoming who they wanted to be, with the love they wanted.

I always felt like I was WAITING. It's not like I *deliberately* put my life on hold — I kept after my career, and I kept up my friends, and I went places and did things...it's just that I felt my *insides* were on hold.

I felt like until I had love and a "permanent" relationship and marriage, I was stuck in some never-never-land.

I wasn't a child, not a girl, and yet — not a woman. Like I had *woman* and *wife* all mixed up.

Now I know better.

I was trying to perfect the WIFE inside me, and what I needed to work on was the WOMAN part.

The whole woman part.

And then I had to learn how to let a man *into* my heart, without giving up my OWN heart, my own HOME, my own SELF. I had to learn to let a man WIND HIMSELF around me, protecting the "pearl" of me, nourishing it, worshipping it, loving it, wanting it — and ME — always.

And now I have that, and it wasn't because I went *looking* for it. I have that because I *allowed* it to happen.

So — let's try to make this a fanciful Tool — BE HIS PEARL.

How can you be the kind of woman that a man treats like a pearl, like a precious, beautiful object to be adored and loved?

What are the qualities of a Pearl?

Beautiful, shiny, glowing, translucent, expensive, absolutely unique, one-of-a-kind, in a relationship with a clam, and BUILT UP IN LAYERS.

A pearl is sort of SPUN.

It starts as a grain of sand, and then gets built bigger and bigger as a part of how the clam responds to the irritation of the grain of sand.

So — the easy thing here is to call him the clam and you the pearl — but that's how we ALL run into TROUBLE.

Let's say, instead, that you are BOTH the pearl AND the clam!

So, you house yourself, you create yourself, you protect yourself, you open your clamshell to the water, to the view, and you allow a man into YOUR WORLD.

Open your clamshell, and allow a man IN.

Now — imagining yourself in this lovely "Pearl" place, allow an imaginary man to take you out into the ocean of the world, and to worship, adore, protect and honor you for the gorgeous, unique, special, one-of-a-kind, delicate Pearl you are (Hey — let's make ourselves pearls with fins and wings — so we can swim and fly — like a "Modern Siren") — and then to let you float back to your shell, so he can be WITH you — without TAKING YOU OVER.

Try to feel some of the translucent qualities of the Pearl-of-You.

***Imagine that you're transparent — that the white, pink or yellow color of your pearl is your substance, your heart, your groundedness — and that, still, anyone can see straight through to your heart.

*** Imagine the "roundness" of the Pearl-of-You so you can "roll" with the water, the wind, the air currents, without digging in and hiding – imagine rolling with your FEELINGS.

***Now imagine a great man HOLDING you, his arms around You-as-Pearl with his heart just FULL of appreciation, admiration, thrills for you.

Just imagine how amazed and thrilled he is to have you next to him, and how hard he's willing to work to be near you.

***Imagine that you are ENDLESSLY FASCINATING to him (you truly are).

***Imagine that he's HAPPY when he's with you, and UNHAPPY when he's not.

***Imagine that he's found his heart in YOU – in YOUR pearl, in You-as-Pearl – in your UNIQUENESS.

I love this image. It makes me feel all sort of soft and smooth and desirable — and a bit mysterious and sought-after, too.

I'm going to pull out a pearl bracelet I have and wear it today — if you have a pearl anywhere in your jewelry box, wear it or put it in your pocket or purse today — and let me know how this feels for you.

These are the kinds of visualizations and flights of imagination that make extraordinary changes in our love lives.

Can you feel how your whole body changes when you think of yourself as a pearl? How you just automatically FEEL more like a girl? More "Leaned Back" and feminine?

Well — this is actually MAGICAL — because it completely shifts your vibe and sends out a signal into the world that makes every man instantly notice you and DESIRE YOU.

A man won't be compelled to nurture you and your heart if he senses a vibe that's hard, masculine, forceful or needy. He won't fall for you because you have wonderful conversations skills or because you're great at giving him advice.

A man's deepest desire won't turn "on" because you're great in bed or because you're prettier than any woman he knows.

BUT...A man is utterly mesmerized by you when you're fully in your Feminine self — Soft on the Outside, Strong on the Inside. When you're self-assured and know and believe in your worth.

Let me know how you feel being a Pearl — and let me know, too — how much more attention and affection you get when you do this Tool.

2

Be His Safe Harbor

$\mathcal{I}$f you just can't seem to get close enough to the man you want in a way that makes him feel BONDED to you...

Or if he and every man you meet seem to be "busy" and thinking about all kinds of things except YOU, I can help.

There's a way to create an unbreakable bond with a man — and that is by making him feel SAFE with you in an emotional sense.

Once you create this kind of safety for a man, where he can be safe to FEEL things with you, there is simply no other woman on Earth who can ever take your place in his heart.

Have you ever felt like life is "dry" and full of just "getting through," and that your man is so caught up in his worries?

Here's the thing:

We are ALL of us, women and men, too — DESPERATE for EMOTIONAL connection.

We're desperate to FEEL — with this essential detail: We're desperate to feel something besides FEAR.

Everything in the world today — everything we read and hear Triggers us — either to terror, or to hope (and that feeling of hope is often simply the flip side of terror for us — we feel backed into a corner and it's either despair or hope, so we bounce from one to the other).

But, what if we could provide a man with EMOTION that would make him feel GOOD — so he doesn't have to live in fear AT ALL — at least when he's with US?

Wouldn't that be a terrifically ATTRACTIVE thing for us to be able to do, easily — almost automatically, and INSTANTLY?

What if WE could be a man's SAFE PLACE. His Safe Harbor — the place where he WANTS to be to recharge himself and feel good — without having his fear Triggered?

Where he feels both safe and yet CURIOUS.

Intrigued by the MYSTERY of what a woman's emotions can do for HIM.

Excited by the idea of where WE ARE — so much so that he wants to go WITH us.

Just imagine this:

Imagine a fabulous man being both intrigued and excited by you, by a sense of mystery and this deep emotional quality we women have that he doesn't own inside himself — AND at the same time feeling loved, totally accepted, not judged and SAFE — so HE can let loose HIS emotions in your presence.

Let's do this. You can — this is supreme femininity. Inner Strength and Outer Softness — and you can DO it.

Here's a Tool — Your Heart In His Computer — to help:

1. In your mind — understand how this is going to work.

A man's mind is like a computer — and so is YOURS.

Thoughts tick along, fragments of thoughts are followed around in a bunch of different directions, thoughts spin...

...and with every tick and spin, we get further and further away from our ESSENCE as a woman.

Our ESSENCE, our souls, who we are inside, isn't something we or anyone else can know all at once.

It takes more than a lifetime to explore and discover and experience and enjoy all the facets of who we are.

And yet, as we do discover, baby-step by baby-step, who we are — as we uncover our essence bit by bit, we have two choices.

We can either clamp down on our discoveries because, yeah, it's all scary — or we can learn to express everything we learn about who we are.

We can learn to provide the good EMOTIONAL connection a man needs (and WE need) – or we can keep doing what we've been doing.

2. The next step is to know the difference between creating SAFETY with our emotions, and creating FEAR with our emotions.

You already know from my ebook and programs about the "Energy Exchange" and how easy it is to push a man away or to simply "turn him off" by Leaning Forward.

Learning to LeanBack is the first, most crucial step – because it sort of "resets" your system and interrupts your old patterns when they're trying to repeat themselves.

Leaning Forward with a man creates FEAR. It makes him tense.

And here's the HIDDEN WAY we Lean Forward – when we're on purpose HIDING our ESSENCE.

When we're Feeling something we don't want to feel, in a man's presence, and so we clamp down on the feeling and pretend not to feel it — or we react to our fear of the Feeling even more strongly — by being defensive, angry, and just generally throwing the energy of the feeling out of our own bodies and onto him — in a verbal attack, or even a tiny, itty bitty "suggestion," we automatically become TENSE.

And the moment we're tense — it makes our man feel FEAR.

He doesn't know what it is — but it makes him lean further away on the couch or at dinner, it makes him not call, it does the opposite of ATTRACT him.

3. SHARE your emotions with your man in a way that conveys these two things:

* You are comfortable with YOUR OWN feelings. And so...

* You are comfortable with HIS feelings.

Now — this automatically creates BOTH Safety AND excitement!

How can that be?

Simple.

When you tell a man, or show a man, or demonstrate to a man that you love him by "caring about" him, and his "issues" and his "troubles" – when you're "nurturing" and "giving" and "attentive" – he feels trapped.

He didn't like that kind of stuff from his mother either, and he CERTAINLY doesn't like it from YOU.

Oh – he'll TAKE everything you give to him – and it will just make him RUN AWAY FROM YOU emotionally.

But when you show a man, and demonstrate to him that you can feel YOUR feelings, that you love and embrace them, and that you're COMFORTABLE and OKAY with your feelings in a non-judgmental way – then – he thinks you're a MIRACLE.

He finds you strong and fascinating, and so DEEP with all your emotional abilities, and that just makes him KNOW that HE can be SAFE with you in an emotional sense.

This creates an unbreakable bond with a man. It puts Heart into his mental computer.

YOUR HEART.

There is simply not another woman on the planet who could ever compete with you once you have this connection with a man.

This is the same kind of CHARISMA we adore in movie stars.

When tears run down a movie star's cheeks in a film, and we FEEL the feelings in ourselves — when it moves US — we're instinctively, powerfully drawn to them.

It's the same with us and a man.

We become like this movie star — charismatic and irresistible.

It makes absolutely no difference what we look like, or what our "personality" is like. Nothing on the "outside" makes a bit of difference to a man who's desperate — as ALL men are — for the EMOTIONAL connection he's missing.

YOU will be that missing connection.

We are ALL — just because we're WOMEN — the ONLY way a man can connect to his deepest self. We're the only way he can open up, the only way he can feel truly safe and truly loved.

And we've all been taught to go AGAINST all the parts of ourselves that make a man feel loved, accepted, and so excited to be around us that he can't wait to call us, see us, and claim us forever.

Instead, we've all been taught to do things that absolutely do not work.

You can instantly switch from all those old, dried-up, masculine, predictable things we're so used to doing to try to get a man's attention, and REALLY, TRULY draw a man in close so he feels compelled to be with you. − start from your OWN ability to feel and Express feelings about YOU and your surroundings − and then see how a man will OPEN UP − effortlessly.

Let me know how this works for you...

3

The Desperation Cure

*I*f love feels like a maze to you — an endless labyrinth with no possible way to get to the center — and, if you're feeling like I once did, that there's not even a prize waiting for you there anyway, I can help you.

When I was at my lowest, all I knew to do was to keep DOING stuff. I was flailing around, chasing after my dreams and chasing after men — as if they were the same thing!

And they're NOT. When I discovered that, and started letting men chase ME while I was busy chasing my DREAMS — everything changed for me.

If you're feeling desperate about your relationship...

If you're feeling the pain and frustration of a relationship that feels like it's going nowhere, with a man who changes his mind every day, and confuses and angers you so much your head is spinning trying to keep track of what's going on and turn things in the right direction, you're not alone.

Know that we have all been through that, and some of us are going through that right now, and I truly want you to know that you DON'T HAVE to go through that.

If I can change my life so instead of waking up every day to despair and desperation — I wake up looking forward to everything terrific I EXPECT to come my way — I KNOW YOU can.

Let's try a simple Tool to help: UNFOLD YOURSELF -

1. Imagine that you're a piece of paper.

2. Imagine that you've allowed a man, or many men, over time, to crumple you up.

3. Imagine that you're all crumpled up in a ball, all stiff and wrinkled and sitting in the middle of an empty room on a cement floor.

4. Imagine a breeze blows, and it rolls you across the floor.

5. Imagine how all that feels.

Let your senses kick in — notice how it feels to be folded up, with your head down, feeling like ANYTHING could blow you across the floor — a breeze, or a man blowing on you.

6. Imagine a man blowing on you and sending you across the room.

What does that feel like?

If you can — write down how it feels, using "Feeling Messages" (my ebook explains how to start using Feeling Messages, and then Modern Siren demonstrates how it works with a man).

Are you getting MAD yet?

I sure am!

Who wouldn't be angry, being crumpled into a ball and blown around the floor by a man!

And yet — that's what so many of us allow to happen.

I remember allowing what I can see now as the most humiliating things to happen — and at the time I thought I was being "honest," or "nice," or "understanding," or "loving."

But I was just crumpled up in a ball, getting blown around.

So — let's DO something about it!

7. Stop Rolling. Sit up in your chair and stop rolling. If your thoughts and feelings are going to a particular man, or to a yearning for ANY man — stop that thought and feeling from rolling, just for a moment, and bring it back, into your body.

Bring it DOWN, inside your body.

Let it roll around inside YOU.

8. Now — UNCRUMPLE yourself. UNFOLD yourself.

* Move your arms out to the sides.

* Move your arms backwards a bit, and feel the weight of them in the middle of your back.

* Feel how you're supporting yourself sitting up.

* Unfold ALL of you — just imagine your energy field opening up — spread your legs, move your hips, stand up, shake yourself out.

Doesn't that feel better?

9.   Keep track of when you're crumpling yourself up.

Anytime you're pining after a man, and working hard to resist calling him or reaching out to him somehow — see if you feel crumpled up inside.

And then — Unfold yourself.   Be dramatic. Stretch yourself out.   Breathe.

And — HOW WILL THIS HELP YOU WITH A MAN?

First, you won't be calling and reaching out to him, you'll be unfolding yourself and finding your bearings again.

You'll have a moment to breathe and a second to do something for YOU — something that feels GOOD — and that has nothing to do with HIM — or ANY man.

Second — he'll feel you unfolding.

He'll feel you from across the table at dinner, or across the room at a party, or across town on the phone, or perhaps even across the country, late at night, when you choose to unfold yourself, turn your attention AWAY from HIM, and turn it where it belongs — on yourself.

Try Unfolding Yourself the next time you talk to ANY man — check out if this particular man makes you fold up and crumple inside, or if you feel like a beautiful, unfolded, soft, waving in the wind piece of gossamer paper that has treasures written all over it.

I KNOW you're BOOKS FULL of treasures — Let me know what you discover about the men around you and the new way they relate to you when YOU know what a treasure trove you are.

4

Be His Juice

Sometimes, even after just a few dates with a man, we can start to feel bonded to him, and when he doesn't seem to care as much as we do, it's so painful. I know. I've been there plenty — and I don't want you to ever have to experience that awful feeling again.

If you feel like the juice has just dried up in your love life — as if all his affection and tenderness just vanished into all the "stuff" he has to do, and all the other "things" in his life, and the "space" he "needs" — it can feel like you're shriveling up.

It feels like HE'S the "juice" in your relationship — and he's not pouring any for you anymore.

This is just so common and upsetting – and there IS a way to turn it around.

First off – he's NOT the juice – YOU are.

Just like a car can't run without gas (or electricity or SOME power source) a relationship can't run without EMOTION.

SOMEBODY in the relationship has to "carry" the emotions in a relationship – and if it's him, you'll be miserable and exhausted working overtime to make him happy and take care of his feelings and row the boat.

What if NEITHER of you are "carrying" the emotions – but just sort of getting along and going along and spending time and going places...?

It sounds pleasant and promising – but it isn't.

If both of you are in your "heads" all the time, thinking – your relationship simply can't GO anywhere. It's stuck in neutral gear. It's got the parking brake on. It won't move.

If YOU, however, can FEEL your feelings – feel how DEEP you are as a woman, then a man can RELAX.

He can feel taken care of and safe — because he knows and feels that YOU have this emotion thing covered, that you can handle it, that you can FEEL — and so he starts letting his guard down.

He starts feeling OKAY letting you see how HE feels.

Until YOU supply that "juice" — he'll just stay in parking gear!

So — what does JUICE look like?

It really doesn't LOOK like anything special or amazing — it just FEELS like emotional energy.

Now — I want to be totally clear here — emotional energy is NOT the same as "drama."

"Drama" is what we do when we're uncomfortable with our feelings, and so we ACT OUT of our RESISTANCE to feeling our feelings.

In other words — if you're angry — but you're not comfortable enough with your deep anger to say "I feel angry" to a man — then you're likely to be dramatic about telling him how wrong he is, or correcting him, or doing or saying something out of anger — instead of simply sharing with him how you feel.

It's this SHARING of your Feeling State that provides the juice in your relationship.

AND — juice doesn't have a LABEL — like "positive" or "negative."

There isn't a rule about whether anger is "negative" and laughing is "positive."

As a human being, as women, we have ALL those feelings going on.

If you're finding yourself ALWAYS angry with a man — that's your clue that something is wrong. You're likely DOING too much. You're likely putting out way too much effort, and pretty much rowing the boat.

So — let's FIND THE JUICE:

Next time you're with a man, instead of working to be perky and funny, and easy and confident — check in with your body and your heart.

How do you REALLY feel?

Are you nervous? Excited? Upset with him about something he just did or didn't do?

The moment you try to pretend you DON'T feel what you actually DO feel − all your juice dries up.

So −

1. Find the juice. Find your feeling, whatever it is. If you have lots of feelings, and they're bounding back and forth, find them all as you can sense them.

2. Write them down. For each feeling, write it like this:

I feel… (sad, mad, glad, afraid…).

3. Now − feel your FACE.

That's right, your face. Put your hand to your cheek and your jaw, and see if you can feel the muscles and how they're working.

See if your face has the same expression as your feelings − see if they match.

That means − if you're smiling − you'd better be feeling happy.

And if you're frowning, you'd better be feeling mad or sad.

4. Now — adjust your face to fit your feelings, instead of the other way around. You may have to excuse yourself and go to the bathroom to check this out in the mirror.

5. Now — take a chance and speak exactly how you're feeling, simply and clearly, without mentioning him or what he did or didn't do.

Try this Tool right now, and let me know how it works for you...

5

Be His Anchor

$\mathcal{I}$f your relationship has lost its fire, and your man has stopped calling like he used to and wanting to see you like he used to, if he's stopped wanting to cuddle on the couch and just hangs out on the computer or the gym or with his friends or even watching sports alone, I know how awful that feels.

If your man has lost his motivation to take your relationship where you want it to go – and you're not sure what happened – it's not even clear WHEN it happened – you just know you're feeling anxious and disturbed where you used to feel full of joy...you're not alone.

A man ALWAYS pulls back a little – no matter HOW MUCH in love he is.

He always comes in and goes out – like a rubber band, while he works out his feelings and digs deeper to find his ability to go the distance in a real relationship.

And all that would be fine – except it feels like the death of the relationship to us.

And how we handle things when a little bit of distance shows up can make all the difference in whether the distance stops and his rubber band comes back to you, or whether he goes all the way out, slips his rubber hand away from you and never really returns.

It's what we do that can either bring him closer or send him away.

It's what we do that either motivates him to come toward us, or de-motivates him and causes him to drift further and further away.

So here's a Tool to help you let him be a rubber band – BE HIS ANCHOR

1. Understand, as deeply as you can, that a man WILL move close and then step back.

KNOW that the Energy Exchange (you can get this important concept in my Reconnect your Relationship program) — will ALWAYS be shifting and re-arranging — but that — NO MATTER WHAT — it's YOUR job to be Leaning Back MOST of the time.

This means, you have to be steadfast on the end of his rubber band that's emotionally ATTACHED to you.

If he starts pulling away, and you move TOWARD him — you're just letting the rubber band go SLACK.

You're making it IMPOSSIBLE for him to bounce back to you — you're eliminating the TENSION he needs in order to come back.

So — you have to ANCHOR his rubber band. You have to KEEP the tension going and keep his attachment to you strong.

We women have been taught the exact opposite thing — we've been taught to move forward when he steps back — and when we do that — we LOSE our Anchor Position.

He'll just end up running away from us CONSTANTLY in order to try to stretch out his rubber band — and if we keep chasing, trying to make it "easy" for him, trying to get close — he'll just get frustrated and take his rubber band away entirely.

It'll just slip away entirely.

2. Learn to ANCHOR.

Practice this. Put one foot behind the other, plant yourself, and Lean Back. Now...

Imagine your man (or a beautiful man you might meet at a party or an event) right in front of you — and imagine him talking to another woman, walking around, talking on the phone, smiling at you and coming toward you, then backing up again and talking to another woman or a man...

Notice everything you're feeling, and everything your body wants to do.

Notice how you INSTINCTIVELY want to move forward, towards him.

It's as though his rubber band is pulling you off balance.

Now — practice standing strong, while being in the Rori Raye Dance Position at the same time. (the full Dance Position — with even more Body Language Tools around it — is in my Commitment Blueprint program — for now, just relax your body in bits and pieces, breathe, and stay Leaning Back)

Imagine that you're ANCHORING his rubber band — and that you have to be strong to keep the tension going (and to not fall over when he comes back toward you and the tension disappears!)

3. Practice Anchoring everywhere you go.

This is the self-esteem, inner strength, "Boundary" part of my entire Rori Raye Method, and so it's only part of the combo of Strong on the Inside, Soft on the Outside.

When you learn how to be Strong on the Inside but Soft on the Outside, you strengthen your inner boundaries.

Once you've "anchored" a man when he's pulling away, you can dive deep into your feelings and (while remaining anchored) share them with a man using Feeling Messages.

So practice Anchoring with everyone you talk to, meet, or even have eye contact with — while you're using Feeling Messages at the same time.

Be sure to let me know how this feels for you...

6

Be His Honey

$\mathscr{J}$f you're struggling in your love life, I know how that feels, and you don't have to go through that pain.

It's not that relationships are simple — your man is a completely different person from you, and men are so different from women, and a romantic relationship brings up all the garbage and bliss of our entire lives along with the pain and joy that's happening with him right now — but that the ways to GET the love you want are simple once you know what you're doing.

Have you ever felt like your man doesn't appreciate you?

Like he could as easily be with you as play sports, or watch TV, or hang with his friends? Or even WORK?

It doesn't have to be like that.

You can MESMERIZE a man, so that he ALWAYS wants to be around YOU – no matter what his other options are.

Today's Tool is about getting a man to want to STICK to you – like glue, like HONEY – in a way that feels good to you.

So – what are the qualities of honey?

Honey is translucent. You can almost see through it – and you can actually see INTO it.

It feels silky and gooey and juicy and solid and thick and sticky.

It smells like flowers and plants and a meadow, and it smells sweet.

It has medicinal healing qualities — honey works like an antibiotic on the skin and can heal skin problems and medical problems where modern antibiotics fail.

It soothes.

It sweetens.

It ATTRACTS — because it's so delicious and valuable and nourishing.

Most important — honey has its own qualities.

Honey is what honey is. It doesn't pretend to be something else. It's not packaged up so it won't be messy.

Honey is honey — it's not processed, distilled, homogenized, pasteurized, and it doesn't disappear.

When you mix Honey into something — you taste the honey.

You know it's there. It makes a statement.

It has a unique fragrance and taste that can't be disguised in a beverage or a jam.

You ALWAYS know something has honey in it.

And it changes with the temperature -
If it's cold, it gets hard and makes crystals on top.
If it's hot, it gets more and more liquid and flows.

SO HOW DOES THIS RELATE TO YOU AND A MAN?

Honey is about ATTRACTION.

Honey is an ultimate attractor, because when you are attracted to honey, and get close to it and touch it – you STICK to it.
You become immersed in it, you revel in it, you want to coat yourself in it.

We women haven't been called "Honey" throughout time for nothing.

We're all those things honey is — nourishing, healing, silky, messy, soothing, sweet and absolutely unique and special.

Think about it...you and I can get emotionally "hot" or go emotionally "cold."

We can get all tight and hard and thick, or we can go soft and FLOW.

We can be sticky and sweet and runny and messy and all about the honey we are and gloriously sexy — or we can freeze ourselves.

We can gloss ourselves over and try to "refine" ourselves so the qualities we have are "played down" and "homogenized" and "pasteurized" — we can try to take the honey qualities OUT of ourselves so we're more like white sugar and not so recognizable...(sweet, but not memorable) — OR we can be ourselves and let our honey qualities shine through.

We can actually DEPEND on our honey qualities.

We can LOVE our honey qualities.
So try this:

1. Imagine yourself as sticky, gooey, soft, flowing, golden honey.

2. Lay down on a bed or the floor or across a chair or couch — and imagine yourself just flowing and glowing and being sticky and melty and sweet and gooey all over it.

3. Breathe into where you feel yourself stuck or tense, and just imagine the honey flowing down your arms, down onto the bed or floor or chair.

4. Relax your pelvis, and imagine the honey pooling in your pelvis, just flowing and glistening and sparkling with vibrant, nurturing, healing energy — for you and for any man who comes near.

5. Carry this feeling around with you all day, and see if it relaxes you and allows you to feel how SPECIAL you are.

I'll be being in my "honey" state all day today right along with you, so let me know how you feel — and what men you attract!

7

Be His ONLY

$\mathcal{I}$f you're feeling resentful, frustrated and upset because your man isn't giving you the attention you deserve – this Tool will help you.

I know what it's like to feel you're not the number one thing on his mind and the ONLY woman in his heart – and we don't want to let that feeling "run" you – so let's turn it around.

Have you ever felt "ordinary"?

Like you can't really understand, on a deep level, what the fantastic man of your dreams would see in you – and that makes you feel angry?

I know exactly what that feels like because it's the way we women have all been *taught* to feel – like we're just "one" woman in a sea of women, and that all women are our competition, and that there's nothing really "special" about us.

And so we have to go to great lengths with hair, makeup, clothes, and "personality" to somehow "stand out from the crowd" and "hold onto our man."

Well — THAT'S JUST NOT TRUE!

Men don't think like that.

Yes — men are "visual," and yes, it's important for us to look good and smell good and sound good — but anything beyond enjoying decorating ourselves, and sensually enjoying our OWN selves is UNNECESSARY!

Really — the whole point is not to become a Barbie doll.

The whole point is to be OURSELVES. To put our "essence" — who we really are deep down — on our outsides, so a man can EXPERIENCE our "specialness."

Our specialness is NOT something we CREATE.

Our specialness is who we ARE.

Every wart and freckle and pound and curve and mistake and feeling.

Our specialness is even who we are when we don't LIKE who we are.

Yes, this is pretty profound. YOU are pretty profound.

I'm saying that a man may ADORE a part of us that WE think is UGLY!

So — if he's going "cold" — or creating distance, or paying attention to other women — is he saying that he's "just discovered the parts of us that we were trying to hide, and didn't like them"?...

Or is he perhaps saying that he's MISSING the parts of us that we're STILL trying to hide?

The more we try to hide because we want to show our "best face" and our best "personality" and our "best body," the more we try to emotionally and literally "keep the lights off," the less interesting we become.

A man can't fall in love with a PICTURE of you — he can only fall in love with the REAL you.

And that's what this Tool is — about YOU being the ONLY.

Now — a lot is made out there about "the One."

The whole "soulmate" concept (which I do NOT agree with).

Well, let's say that it were true — that everyone's out there looking for the "one" — the true soulmate.

How exactly could a man find out if you were his "One" if he can only see the parts of you that you WANT to show him?

He can't.

So — try this right now...

1. Get out a piece of paper and write down this first list — **Things about yourself that make you unhappy.** Now...

2. Write a new list with **Things about yourself that not only make you unhappy — but that you COMPLAIN about.** Now, let's go even further...

3. Write a new list with the **Things you actually DISLIKE about yourself. Even "hate."** Now...

4. You have 3 lists — all PAINFUL.

On these lists are everything that you think "If I could just get rid of these things...I'd get the man I want."

On these lists are everything STANDING IN YOUR WAY.

Now...let's reverse things.

But — instead of trying to IMPROVE on these things you find "negative" about yourself, I want you to make a quick decision, for the sake of doing this Tool, that these things on your list are the BEST THINGS about you.

I want you to imagine an alternate sort of universe in which the things you just wrote on your lists are the qualities MOST PRIZED.

How does that feel?

Do you feel a little turned upside down? A little silly?

I mean, it's not often you think of being "messy" and "disorganized" or "30 pounds over my ideal weight" or "angry" as WINNER qualities — but I want you to try imagining it.

If it makes you laugh — great.

5. Now — the last part here is tricky, and I'm going to hold you ACCOUNTABLE for it, so be sure to comment on my blog to let me know how you're doing with this -

http://blog.HaveTheRelationshipYouWant.com

Here it is — I want you to do this OUT IN THE WORLD.

That means, if you drop something in the middle of a date, if you find yourself nervous and laughing too much with a pasted smile on your face, if you catch yourself doing or thinking or FEELING LIKE anything on any of your 3 lists — you'll instantly — SMILE. At YOURSELF.

Then you'll give yourself a quick "thumbs up" — because you've just displayed or expressed or just "lived" one of those PRIZED QUALITIES on your lists.

Please make sure you breathe, in and out deeply at least 3 times, and sink into whatever you feel when you smile at yourself.

So — how is this going to effect HIM?

Pretty majorly. He's going to instantaneously GET that you are unusual, unique, different, fascinating...and most important...

He'll get that YOU feel SAFE being YOURSELF — and instantly feel that he can TRUST YOU to make it safe for HIM to be HIMSELF!

This is very, very different than TRYING to make him feel safe and "nurtured."

You are setting an example for him.

You're showing him that being with you is going to be quite the adventure — and that you're not only UP for it — you're the ONLY WOMAN IN THE WORLD who can TAKE him there.

You are the ONE woman in the world who can offer a relationship with YOU."

And to him, from the moment he feels connected to you with this Tool — YOU are a magical place.

He won't be able to help himself...

He'll feel that you understand him, that you "get" him, that he can relax around you, that you're his "One."

If it seems too good to be true — that you can actually be yourself and actually attract a man more than if you're being attentive, made up, dressed up and sexy on purpose — I promise you it's not too good to be true. It IS true.

It's all the pretending that we do, all the hiding and living with the "lights off" that keeps a man from truly falling for us.

Try this Tool — do your lists, smile at yourself, and be sure to let me know how it goes.

8

Be His Last

*D*o you ever feel like you're just one woman in a long stream of women for any man you really like?

That he's always ready to "move on" from you — and that it's somehow YOUR job to "keep him interested?"

That's how I was taught to be with a man — that any man who wanted me at first would eventually "lose interest" and leave. He'd either leave me for another woman, or he'd leave me for the "last" woman — his ex.

This happened to me so many times — and I know it has for you, too — that I just never knew what it felt like to be "settled" with someone, until I met my husband.

Before, any man who wanted me consistently bored me. I just wasn't interested, and I likely hurt several men by WANTING to want them — but just not really getting there emotionally.

There was one man where we had an instant connection that lasted years — but after the first few months, I was miserable and at his mercy — and STILL stayed, working hard for the relationship, until one morning I just woke up and didn't feel anything for him.

It was an amazing moment, and I was sure it would pass, but it didn't.

He felt like a "roommate" to me — nothing more. It was as though my whole "in love" system had shut down. Done. Over.

And so I left.

It was one of the bravest things I've ever done in my life, and so I know how hard it is if you feel stuck in a relationship where you're just not getting what you need and feel uncertain about his feelings all the time.

And yet — I know that if I had the Tools I have now — things would have been different.

Either the relationship would have turned around, and we would have reconnected and got close again. Or...

I would have known SO MUCH SOONER that I was in the wrong place.

I would have known that I needed and wanted and deserved DEVOTION.

So – I wish this for you – to get a man's devotion – just as you deserve – so that you will no longer be in the middle of his "stream" of women. You will be his LAST woman.

Try this when you're alone (some of it is outrageous and loud):

1. Imagine a man standing in front of you, just about five feet away.

2. Imagine him smiling at you and giving you attention.

3. Now – imagine a bunch of other women walking by him – in between you and him, and

behind him, and walking around him — touching him, smiling at him — and looking at you in a dismissing sort of way.

That's tough to imagine, isn't it? Don't give up!

See if you can stay still, breathe, open your heart and smile, and do the Rori Raye Dance Position. (The whole Dance Position, with some extra parts, is in my Commitment Blueprint program — for now, simply "Ground yourself" by imagining there's a tree trunk going down your back to establish the "Strong on the Inside" part of you, and then imagine there's a big plastic zipper covering your heart up and "Unzipper" your heart, so it's open to any man who's near you, to establish the "Soft on the Outside" part of you.

Okay...now...

4. How do you feel?

* Are you angry at the women, focused on them, or are you simply "Leaning Back" and taking in the energy from the man?

* Are you tense in your body, or open and receiving his attention and smile?

5. Every once in a while, notice that he notices one or two of the other women for a moment, and then turns his attention right back to you.

See how *that* feels in your body...

6. Check out your body from the top of your head to the bottom of your toes, and let every single square inch of you soften and relax by stroking it, talking to it, kissing it, embracing it...allowing it to feel what it feels.

(Remember — every square inch of your body, inside and out, *feels* something.)

* If you're feeling upset — say it out loud "I feel upset."

* If you're feeling angry — say it out loud "I feel angry."

* If you're swooning with passion for this man, say it out loud "I feel so turned on..."

* If you want to run away and curl up and hide from all this pressure from these women and the wondering what he's going to do next — say it out loud "I feel scared and burned out and terrified and I want to go away and hide and not DO this anymore..."

I don't want you to try to control your feelings.

When you're with a man, or hoping to meet a man who you feel attracted to...all kinds of old and new feelings are going to come up.

Old "stuff" is going to be triggered and all of a sudden — without explanation and very uncomfortably — show up.

Anger is going to show up and then guilt, and then fear, and then desire, and then back to fear and then back to anger, and on and on. It's going to bounce around inside you.

Your job is to *let* it bounce!

The problem we all have is trying so hard to keep things the way we want them. The way they started out.

And it will never happen like that.

A relationship either grows closer or it grows farther apart — and most of the time it bounces around between those two. Nothing we can do will keep ANYTHING "the same."

The secret to being a man's "last" is NOT CARING where you fit in his "stream of women."

It's ASSUMING you will be last, should YOU choose to accept that position — and absolutely, thoroughly, totally, completely DENYING any man who isn't thinking that you are the last woman in his life from having control over your time, your life, your heart, your schedule — your LOVE.

So — here's the last step:

7.   Imagine there are hundreds of men wandering around YOU.

They're talking to you, and touching you, and pushing each other out of the way, and walking around you, and walking between you and the man in front of you.

How does THAT feel?

Do you feel angry? Do you feel revengeful? Do you feel peaceful? Do you feel silly? Do you feel scared?

It's really important to try this on — to imagine it deeply and in detail and really, really pay attention to how you feel.

If you can do this often, by yourself — you'll no longer feel at any man's mercy.

You'll feel CONFIDENT.

You'll have an attitude that tells a man that you know you're deserving of his love and devotion, and if you don't get what you need from him, you won't stick around too long.

This attitude is very important, because it tells a man that you're in charge of your own destiny in love — and that is VERY attractive to a man.

9

Be Why He Opens Up

*I*f your man is "uncertain," if he blows hot and then cold, if one minute he wants to live with you and marry you and the next he isn't "sure" about you — I know how devastating that can be.

You don't know whether to be understanding or angry — and you feel everything from pain to frustration to wanting to just give up and walk away.

All of relationship boils down to one thing: ATTRACTION. A man doesn't know what hit him when he FEELS attraction. He can't explain what it is about you he loves — he just loves you. It doesn't matter what you look like, what your personality's like, how you are in bed...nothing matters except that he feels this...Attraction.

If he hasn't said "I love you," and you haven't told him how you feel, either — but it's been a long time, maybe a year, and you're only dating him...what should you do?

The game-playing theory is: Don't say "I love you" first. And generally — it's not a good idea to do ANYTHING "first" with a man — to initiate anything.

But relationships either move forward or they die.

After a year, the chances of your relationship getting to marriage go DOWN, not up...and if he hasn't told you he loves you — he may not love you, or he may just not be able to SAY what he feels.

Either way — at a certain point you have to speak the truth about how you feel — even about HIM.

The old rule about not letting a man know you love him before he lets you know he loves you — works...up to a point.

But the reason it helps is NOT because of the words you're not saying and the affection you're not giving...it's because the restraint required to NOT do and say how you feel automatically makes you LEANBACK a bit.

It makes you RESERVE your energy so that you're not pressuring him.

And at a certain point...to take things to the next level...YOU have to be the one to open things up. And it requires a BIG PICTURE, and some fearlessness.

So let's do that NOW!

To OPEN HIM UP — you have to open YOURSELF up FIRST.

Yep, you have to go first.

And that's going to mean you can't rely on the "game" or the "rules" anymore.

You can't get him to step forward with love for you until YOU open the floodgates.

YOU have to show the way — but in a completely different way than how our old "need and desperation" would do it.

Start here:

1. Get out a piece of paper and a pencil (or pen).

2. Write down something you want from your man, something you want him to OPEN UP about.

Something you want him to be "feminine" about and tell you how he "feels."

3. Now, ask yourself the same question, and write down your answers.

Make it go this way:

Do not talk about him in any way...except as the matter-of-fact that he's participating, that he's there in your experience — like "When you touch me...I feel all tingly inside..." Or...

"When I look in your eyes, I feel myself go all mushy."

"I feel lonely for my childhood home..."

"I feel so happy when I'm with you..."

"I feel so turned on by (fill in the blank here, for example: looking at art at the museum... playing catch with my niece...walking in the woods...reading fantasy novels...)

"I feel a yearning for marriage and family and to have a home with love and warmth..."

4. Now...when you're with him, and things are feeling stuck, and you're afraid to bring up whatever it is you WANT from him...catch yourself.

Stop yourself from asking him what HE'S feeling. (It's always okay to ask him what he WANTS, or what he THINKS...but asking for FEELINGS is very, very different.)

5. Pull out what you've written here with this Tool, and "Speak the Truth" of something YOU feel.

It can be as non-relationship related as your feelings about art exhibits (as long as it's deeply felt and deeply personal) – or it can be about the relationship, just the way you've written it.

Yes, you can say "This feels so good to me, just sitting here with you watching TV."

Yes, you can say "I feel all gooey just looking at your eyes." (As long as you're not distracting him from work or something he's doing, or a ball game on TV.)

You can open up FIRST.

I know this is scary to even think about — so PRACTICE.

I know we all think playing it "cool" is the way to go here — but it's not.

If you have CONFIDENCE — there's no NEED to play it cool!

There is absolutely nothing more attractive to a man than a woman who is confident and independent who is able to turn into jelly in his presence.

A man who feels loved by a woman with a High Degree of Difficulty will open up in an amazing way.

He only needs YOU to lead the way.

He needs to feel the emotionally safety that only YOU can provide — and not by telling him you love him and that he's safe — but by

DEMONSTRATING to him that he's safe with you because YOU feel safe with you.

I know it's asking a lot — to open up before he does — but it won't work if you do it in the old way that reeks of clinginess, need and desperation — and that you WANT something from him.

You have to open up for YOU — simply because your feelings are so amazing that you have to SHARE them.

Let me know how this Tool works for you, and how it feels to Open Up First.

10

Be With Him

$\mathcal{J}$f you're enduring pain and frustration because you're not sure where your relationship is going, and you just want with all your heart for your man to step up, claim you, act like a man and commit to you — I totally know how you feel... and here's some help.

The first clue that you *need* help in your relationship is when love stops being easy -

If you've become "exclusive" with a man before the ring is on your finger and the wedding date is set — how do you handle the ups and downs and insecurities and weirdnesses that come up — the very things that my Circular Dating tools are meant to help you avoid?

There's a firm line between "dating" and "not dating." But Circular Dating embraces a much "grayer" area — and that's how you "relate" to all men, everywhere, even though you're technically "exclusive" with one man.

Here's part of a comment from "J" — and my answer to this part will help you turn that black-and-white way of looking at this into something much better-feeling and more helpful:

"Dear Rori,
...since we've been dating for 8 months and have had marriage, kids, etc on the table as well as our timelines (he told me his timeline for marriage and kids is 6 months later than mine). we have a great relationship...I see myself with him in the future. I love him and he loves me.

My question with exclusivity: I accepted his third request for exclusivity after our talk about it and my agreement of terms. However, after hearing your program, I feel like I should date other people.

I do, however, think this would be painful to him. He's done everything to show me he is invested and loves me (meeting my family several times and me meeting his). I would think he would want to break up if I said I wanted to date other people...since he's been a great man to me.

What if when I say to him, 'you can take all the time you need, I don't want to put pressure on you or on the relationship...I'm just not willing to shut my options down right now' that he'll say, 'Well I want to be with someone who will be true to me and us. I want to know you have the ability to be faithful to me down the road. And this dating other people shows me you can't be and that you might cheat on me in the future.' Then what? Thank you. J"

Here's my answer:

You can Circular Date without actually DATING anyone — just flirting and letting men come up to you and talk with you and EXPERIENCING that your options are open.

It's having the solid confidence that if your man slipped up or got wishy-washy — you'd be able to go out and have fun with a new man at the drop of a hat.

That vibe in you is all you need for now..

So — without trying to give you all the nuts and bolts of Circular Dating that are in my Targeting Mr. Right program, let's just talk here about how this could work in your MIND:

1. Stop Guessing.

There's a BIG thing I hear in your letter — and that's you GUESSING. You're guessing "what he would say" if you were to give him the "No Boyfriend" speech so that he can understand it.

2. Define what YOU mean by "options open."

I'm certain he would not expect that you would not TALK to another man.

Will you feel guilty talking to another man? Flirting with him?

Letting him ask for your phone number or email address?

Giving you his business card?

Or does this feel natural to you under the circumstances?

Everywhere you go, and everything you do, there are men. All sizes, shapes, colors, types...

You can either close yourself and your body down around them, or you can...

3. Keep YOURSELF open.

You can either radiate an "I'm not available in any way" vibe, or you can radiate an "I'm not married — give it your best shot" vibe, or you can radiate an "I'm exclusively involved at the moment, and I plan to be married, yet I'm open to finding out who you are..." vibe.

There's all kinds of ways to be in this world — and closed down is my least favorite.

There's a big difference between having your vibe be completely open and available and actually GOING on a literal "date."

And there's a big difference between having coffee at a coffee shop with a man who just came up to you out-of-the-blue, sat down and started a conversation, and letting him pick you up and take you to dinner.

There's a lot of gray area in there.

4. Embrace the gray area.

In your MIND — see what you can find in that gray area that would work for you.

A gray area you can actually put into words, that you could actually share with the man you're exclusive with. (So you can stop guessing.)

A gray area you can be comfortable with — so that you are always living the Rori Raye Mantra — Trust Your Boundaries, Follow Your Feelings, Choose Your Words, and most important here...

5. Be Surprised.

Your willingness to be surprised, and to be curious about the world around you and the people in it — including men — can be HUGE.

This is ALL Circular Dating.

It's ALL accessing and using the "Diva" part of you that truly lives — 100% — IN the world and doesn't shut down her sensuality and sexuality and feminine vibe under ANY circumstances.

It's about how you can...

6. Be in a state of ROMANCE with the entire world.

Put on your "romance" glasses and see the world through them.

See everything as interesting and romantic, quaint and curious, fresh and inspiring... basically something you can love by just loving yourself in its presence.

Let me know if this letter jogs your thinking around this — and get out in the world and see if you can relate to men in this open way even if you're exclusively involved with one man.

11

Be His Goddess

Are you angry and you don't even know it? So angry in fact, that you're doing everything you know to NOT be angry? I know just what this feels like, because anger is the one emotion that frightens me more than any other.

And yet − it's the POWER of your anger that can make or break your love life − depending on how you're able to USE that power by EXPRESSING yourself in a way that will mesmerize a man, instead of push him away.

Have you ever felt so angry with a man and at the same time so absolutely stuck in a place where you need to be so nice?

When the need to be a good woman, a nice woman, an understanding woman, a

REASONABLE woman completely overpowers what you FEEL? I know exactly what that feels like.

It felt, for me, like I was being pulled in two different directions. I felt like I was on some kind of torture rack.

The moment I thought about how angry I was I would immediately feel so much terror — like if he knew how angry and childish and petulant I was feeling, he'd run from me, and so I had to be very, very careful not to let that out.

I had to be so very careful to be adult and mature and calm and nice.

And the thing is — being nice and understanding and trying to keep my anger under wraps was what drove him away!

I couldn't win.

And you don't have to go through that. It took me a long time of trial-and-error to figure this out, but when I finally did it was like magic came in and took over my life.

Instead of fighting my feelings all the time, I started to embrace my feelings and actually USE them to bring a man closer to me.

And the hardest part of that was how frightening it was.

Because as a man was coming closer to me I realized he could see into me. I realized he could see how angry and petulant and childish I was. I realize he could see my tears. Even if I was trying to hide them.

I realized that the harder I tried to hide all that stuff the more he could see it — but he didn't see it in that pure lovely way that a man experiences our feelings.

He experienced my feelings through this tension and cover-up of trying to be nice — and so he always felt tense around me. He couldn't quite put his finger on it but he never really trusted me. Not any man.

Here I was, being the nicest woman on the planet, and yet making him feel as though I could not be trusted!

How messed up is that!

The first emotion that we have to tackle — to become emotionally "authentic" and get rid of all the old covers over our real feelings and start to use our feelings *for* ourselves instead of *against* ourselves — is ANGER.

Anger is just anger. It's just a feeling. It's just a feeling like any other feeling, except it's kind of exciting.

Anger is the go-to position for a man, because that's the way he's been conditioned. He hasn't been taught to be nice and sweet and demure. He's taught to be competitive. He's taught to fight. He's taught to overpower his competition — and he's rewarded for that!

We, however, as women — and this is what the whole feminist movement has really been all about — is that when we're competitive, we *naturally* want to fight. We want to overpower our competition. We want to WIN! And yet our *training* as women is to NOT be and feel these things, and so we immediately squash ourselves before any of those impulses even get out.

Now, it's so much more acceptable for us to be tough in business. To be strong and successful and even driven. And the thing is — men actually and truly find women who are tough, strong, driven, and successful to be incredibly attractive and sexy.

But we think it's a horrible thing.

And so we shut ourselves down.

The weird and awful part of this is that it doesn't stop there. We don't just successfully squash down all our more masculine impulses – they squeak out of us in all kinds of weird and unpleasant ways.

Because we're not allowing ourselves to be powerful in our life and our business and our work – we feel completely out of control, and so we become all ABOUT control.

We not only want to control everything about our life and work, we want to control everything about our men and our relationships.

And there is just nothing more unattractive than us trying to control everything about our men and our relationships.

Also – there is nothing less feminist about it.

Part of being a successful person is knowing *when* to use *what* skills.

89

We know it's completely inappropriate to want to overpower a man and win him — we know it's completely inappropriate to treat a relationship like a boardroom and try to run everything.

But we still want to.

And until we learn to let those masculine parts of ourselves really fly out in the world where it WORKS — when we're focused on changing the world — we're going to try to wash those feelings down and end up squeaking them out all over our men. And that's when we lose what we want. That's when we lose ourselves.

So here's a tool to start getting in touch with your righteous anger so that we can figure out what to DO with that anger once were feeling it: THE ROCK IN YOUR HAND -

1. Imagine you have a rock in your hand.

In fact, go out and get yourself a pretty little rock — not from a nice little store — but off the ground. Something rough and jagged and mean looking. Keep it in your purse or your pocket.

2. Imagine your man or the man you're interested in or the last man who hurt you.

Imagine holding your rock in your hand. Imagine throwing it at him. Imagine smashing his skull in with the rock. Imagine jumping up and down on him and completely creaming him and throwing the rock at him.

Go ahead and imagine the most gruesome and grotesque things you WANT to do with your anger around him.

Don't try to be nice. Don't try to be reasonable. Don't try to be mature. You don't have to worry about controlling yourself, because he's not really there and you're not really doing anything at all except imagining.

3. After you let off a little steam and you've let yourself experience the full extent of your anger — pretty powerful isn't it? — put down your arm and just let yourself feel the fullness of this anger that you're feeling.

See if you can feel how less tense your shoulders are right now. How less tense your belly is, how less tense your chest is. See if you can feel how much more open and relaxed your heart is.

Now imagine your rock in your hand again.

Just know you have it. Think of that rock as your reminder that you're a human being. That you have feelings and that anger is something you feel.

4. Now let's process this anger through.

You are angry because:

>>> *1. You've put out too much effort in this relationship.*

You've called, you've texted, you've thought about him too much, you've been sending energy his way that he hasn't been returning.

Remind yourself that this is not about him — he's just doing what he does — this is about you doing TOO much.

>>> *2. You've forgotten about yourself while you've been focused on him.*

Your life has gotten smaller. All of a sudden you're not having so much fun with girlfriends and hanging out by yourself and doing things you normally love.

Work is no longer inspiring. And if it never was inspiring, you've lost interest in getting a better work situation.

There are other reasons for being angry – and yet these are the ones I want to work with now.

These two reasons in step #4 are under our control and we can change what happens around them fast.

Changing these – in baby-steps – will get you a huge result almost instantly.

So – start by investigating how you're putting so much energy out toward a man that it's making you feel angry and resentful, and how you're neglecting yourself –

As you slowly stop putting energy out, and slowly put your energy onto yourself, instead, you'll feel stronger, feel more powerful, and *get his interest back.*

12

Be His Air

*I*f you never seem to get what you deserve in a relationship — or even on a date — where you feel like you have to put out effort or nothing will happen, where you have to work to get your needs met, I know how awful that feels.

It feels like you're "in this alone." I remember what that felt like, and I don't want you to have to suffer like I did. If you're with a man — you feel both trapped exclusively with him, and with no way to get your needs met. And if you're dating, you feel like no man "gets" you.

Do you ever feel like the more you give, the less you get back?

And the less you get back, the worse you feel — to where you start feeling unsure of yourself with him, then insecure all the time, then needy — on to even actually desperate to get the relationship back to where you were?

It's like an equation — The more we give, plus the less we get back equals how desperately unhappy we feel.

I remember being the queen of giving — it made me feel good to give to a man (my time, my energy, my money, my love for him...).

But I mostly remember not getting anything back — not what I wanted, not what I needed, not what I hoped for, and definitely not what I deserved.

I remember not getting my needs met, and I remember feeling bad almost all the time — except for those few moments that felt good — you know what I mean.

Almost all of us have felt exactly like this with a man we like. And many of us are feeling it RIGHT NOW.

If this is happening to you — which of these three things are you doing? Are you:

1. Stuffing all of it down and acting 'cool'

2. Stuffing a little of it down and trying to find a middle range of how to act, even though you may feel like climbing all over him. Or...

3. Abandoning yourself to the feelings, and CHASING him down.

It really hurts when we don't get back what we put out.

And it's really frustrating to know that just PUTTING OUT that kind of energy is enough to drive most any man AWAY.

Even knowing, down deep, and in the back of our minds, that showering our man with love and affection doesn't work, we feel COMPELLED to keep doing it.

And the more it doesn't work, the further away he goes and the more we feel compelled to give.

Giving seems to be the right thing to do —
even when we can see and experience and feel for
ourselves that it isn't working.

And then we give more and more — and as
soon as we continue doing that — we are
ABSOLUTELY SURE to GET EVEN LESS
FROM HIM!

Lillian wrote to me with just this situation:

"Dear Rori, You talk about how we women tend to
chase or 'pick up the slack' in a relationship like it's a
rubber band...and it's so true, but I don't know how
to stop myself. It's just so...natural to do things like:

I'll meet a man I like, and we strike up a
conversation and so I'll tell him I'll email him with
some info or something that maybe he wanted, or
just mentioned. I just did that with this man I met at
a party...so I emailed him, and he DIDN'T email me
back — until several days later...and then it was just a
thank you sort of dry thing...and then, so, of course, I
emailed him again, I mean, it just seemed like the
'right' thing to do — to be chatty and 'follow up' with
him...

I guess I just go crazy if I can't DO something — especially in this day and age when we're all supposed to be so 'equal' — and a man expects me to at least meet him 'half-way...'

I don't understand what's giving a man 'space' and what's 'not showing interest' — and I can't tell the difference between chasing a man and just being 'normal.' Help, Lillian"

Nearly everything we're told to do around men is so wrong, including things like:

1. We can ask a man out, we can follow up, we can just ask him if he's interested in us. It's the 21st century and we can be "just like the men"

2. We should be the ones who make the effort to get our man interested in romance, we need to seduce him, we need to make plans for romantic nights out, etc.

The truth is, it's just totally against our nature as women to do these kinds of things. It changes our vibe, it changes our energy, it changes our chemistry inside ourselves so that it changes our muscles and − it changes the EXPRESSION on our FACES!

So, when you're tempted to do these kinds of things − KNOW that you're stuck in your head and in an old place that is NOT good for you.

What you want to be is INDESPENSIBLE to a man.

You want to be as NECESSARY to him as food, water and air.

You want him to not feel "right" without you around.

Can you see how this is completely different from going around "offering yourself" to him?

Even dressed up to look like a "modern woman thing," playing the man's part of working out relationship details is actually a "desperate woman thing," − and I don't want you stuck there.

I want you to BE what a man needs − just because you ARE what he needs!

I want you to simply TRUST that you ARE what he needs.

So, to be the air he NEEDS to BREATHE — first YOU have to BELIEVE you ARE. And the FASTEST way to make that happen is to start here with this Tool:

BREATHE IN AND OUT THROUGH YOUR HEART.

There are all kinds of breathing techniques out there that will help you slow down, calm down, feel better and stronger.

Some breathing exercises are meditations, some require counting, some, like some in yoga, require moving.

"Breathing in and out through your heart" just focuses your attention on YOURSELF — which is a huge part of Loving Yourself (which, as you know, is very important in our work together).

It's easy.

Just imagine that your breath is coming in from the outside world and into your body THROUGH YOUR HEART.

You don't have to do anything − no counting, no thinking − just imagine it.

And then, when you feel your body naturally breathe out, imagine it coming OUT through your heart.

Just do it for a few seconds.

It will calm down your system, and give you a moment to − physically, emotionally, energetically, and in every other way − Leanback.

And the moment you Leanback, you will have a moment to CHOOSE what to do next.

And if what you want is to bring your man closer to you, you might choose to put down the phone, move away from your email, and shift your thoughts from your man to YOURSELF.

I know changing the way we naturally want to do things is a lot for me to ask.

It's easy for me to say JUST PUT DOWN THE PHONE, JUST DON'T EMAIL HIM AGAIN.

But — if you can do it ONCE, just once, you'll see.

You'll see that it's NOT THAT HARD.

You'll feel empowered, just like I did.

And instead of feeling out of control, like Lillian, you'll feel a new sense of being in charge of yourself (which is very different from being in charge of HIM).

So, to summarize this Tool — it's about an important part of the Rori Raye Mantra (you can get it free with your free newsletter subscription):

The Mantra goes: Trust Your Boundaries, Follow Your Feelings, Choose Your Words, Be Surprised — and the part this Tool will help you with is following your feelings and choosing your words.

So next time you feel compelled to pick up the phone or tell him you love him, STOP.

Breathe in and out through your heart.

Ask yourself if you care whether or not he returns you love, your hug, your kiss, your call, or your email.

If the answer is "Yes, I do care," then you know what to do — and what to NOT do.

I know you can do this. For today, just practice breathing through and with your heart, and you'll automatically start seeing things go differently for you with the man you want.

What we're talking about here is ATTRACTION. Attracting a man so deeply and powerfully that he'll do almost anything to get close to you.

It's a completely different feeling than that tense and anxious sense that WE have to DO something in order to attract him — it's the calm certainty of knowing that we are NATURALLY so attractive that nearly EVERY man will want to get close to us.

It's about being the air HE NEEDS in order to breathe — the woman he will NOT be WITHOUT.

The way to a man's heart is through your OWN heart. The way to make a man fall in love with you is to first fall in love with yourself.

Start with Breathing Through Your Heart, and let me know how this Tool helps you

13

Be His Healing

ere's a situation — a VERY common situation — where a man is consistently defensive and on the attack in order to feel okay with himself. The cure is in my Toxic Men program, and I'll touch on it here.

It's about unearthing the anger in you, in him, in the relationship, and getting it out in the open in a NON-DRAMATIC way, so it can be healed — and USED — to bring you closer to each other.

Otherwise, the anger goes underground and does so much damage there that things are seemingly beyond repair — but it IS repairable. The key is in YOU.

SOMEONE has to start a new kind of communication, a new kind of attitude and approach, a new way of expressing all kinds of feelings — both verbally and physically — that actually CREATE INTIMACY, instead of driving it away.

To do this — you need more strength on the inside — more trust in yourself to state clearer, more consistent Boundaries — and a willingness to be completely vulnerable on the outside.

You have to trust yourself that you will not just BE there, vulnerable and open, when things don't feel good — when there is even "modest" defensiveness and verbal abuse (I was with a man for a long time who was master of verbal abuse and manipulation — he was funny and charming, and so everyone always laughed, and I stood there wondering what was wrong with me...).

You have to know how to always stay open, and yet always feel strong enough to walk away. At any moment. That's Power....

Here are 2 symptoms that anger is underground and running things:

1. Judgment and Criticism — you always feel as though everything you do is being "watched' and "scrutinized" and "judged."

Every time you do anything, he's ready with a roll of his eyes, a snide comment — about what you did, about what you didn't do, about his own needs that somehow it's your fault aren't being met (like where things are).

Sometimes it's about simple choices you make — or how you look or what you're wearing. Sometimes it's loud, sometimes it's muttered, sometimes it's done with a joke (so it's even harder for you to pin down). It's constant and never-ending. You feel like a child being berated.

This is about a lot of things, but it can simply be the most "controlled" way a man can express his anger (often his anger at himself — it might have nothing to do with you). He judges you constantly because he's such a harsh judge of himself. His guilt about his irritation and anger leaves him this "mild" way to express anger — telling you what you're doing wrong.

(By the way — we do this too...)

2. Withdrawing

He's drifting away emotionally, spending less time with you, there's less sex, less affection.

Almost all my programs deal with this and how to stop it and bring him close again — and here — let's just look at the hidden anger component: He's angry, he doesn't know how to deal with it, and so he withdraws. It's easier.

When you talk with him and try to be "understanding" and get at what the problem is — *he just feels angrier, and withdraws more.*

The obvious expression of anger is arguments, fighting, verbal and physical attacks — but I don't want to deal with that here because this is about HIDDEN anger — where all you're experiencing is the tip of the iceberg, and you're living in fear of that iceberg surfacing.

And here's a small step to the solution: Unearth the anger iceberg by YOU changing YOUR reactions.

Now — this is not a lifestyle. You don't want to be with a man who is constantly berating you or withdrawing from you where you have to be the one always "changing" — this is an experiment, a test, a learning experience. And the goal here is just to unearth the anger and learn to TOLERATE the experience of it.

Once you can get through surface stuff and into the rage that lies underneath — without all the arguing and fighting and nastiness that only uncovers a tiny part of the iceberg and actually DAMAGES a relationship — you'll start to feel things loosen up and more affection, attention and love start to fill the space between you.

What you want to do is — instead of running away, or making an excuse for yourself or DEFENDING yourself — you want to:

1. Notice what's going on with you. Are you being run by fear? Do you want to run away? Do you want to hit him? Are you going numb? Are you determined to do whatever you have to, to make peace and get his approval?

2. Speak the DEEPEST feeling you can find inside yourself.

That could be "I feel scared." "I feel so angry." "I feel turned off."

When he questions you, just keep doing what you're doing, saying your deepest feeling. If you have to put it in context, say "When I heard (you can repeat what he said here, or paraphrase it...just enough to let him know what you're referring to...) — "I feel so tense...it felt awful...it feels scary...I felt like running...I feel like running...This doesn't feel good to me..."

3. Stand your ground.

Don't apologize for yourself, explain anything — and do not blame him, either.

Look him straight in the eye, as best you can. Lean back. You are not attacking, you are expressing.

What can you expect with doing it this way? All kinds of stuff will come up for you...

You'll feel shaky, you'll feel upset − and you'll feel ANGRIER than you've ever felt! And what's more...as YOU feel more comfortable with YOUR anger − so will he.

He'll start to let you "have it."

He'll start to let his anger out. And you have to be strong enough to hear anger and experience the ENERGY of anger − AS LONG AS IT'S NOT DIRECTED AT YOU!!

This means − the moment he turns it on YOU − you say "I'm happy to hear your feelings, even your anger, but I don't want to feel attacked..." and if he doesn't change his words and copy what you're doing (expressing his feelings instead of blaming YOU), or doing the masculine energy thing of trying to *fix* the problem in a good-faith, good-feeling way (this is GOOD!), then you must TURN AROUND AND WALK AWAY...!

When this happens, and emotions start to surface, I know it's tough — but, actually — it's fabulous!!! You are starting to communicate in a way that is triggering YOURSELF and your stuffed up and old feelings.

Now — all we have to do is get a routine down for how to handle your emotions when they bubble up...The more you tell him the truth, in feeling messages, the more you will feel that you don't WANT to feel — otherwise you would have done this a long time ago.

Believe it or not — this is amazing PROGRESS. And — ALWAYS — the first emotion that shows up is ANGER.

Accept that you are enraged — and just keep processing it and sharing it. This is going to feel weird for a bit — so it's really important you have a way to relax — to meditate — to regroup and ground yourself. Stuff you love that you can focus on and feel better quickly.

If he's a man who NEEDS to put YOU down in order to feel okay — he won't let up right away.

He's going to up the ante, and keep at you to try to get a "rise" out of you so that you'll go back to the old, crummy defense patterns you used to be stuck in.

He may start to panic, and so he'll do the only thing he knows — attacking you. You're going to have to acknowledge how awful that feels right away — instead of stuffing down and answering him reasonably.

Later on — you'll get a sense of humor about it — and he'll stop doing this very soon...when you start feeling more powerful.

Defending yourself with anger or cleverness will not help you here — it will just make him work harder to top you.

As you express your anger simply, and let him know it doesn't feel good, that you feel attacked, that you feel afraid of him and what he'll say to you, and that it's making you feel turned off...all this will change....You are only at the BEGINNING of this...be patient, take baby steps.

14

Be His Gold

*J*f you're enduring a love life that isn't what you've dreamed of, I KNOW you can have what you want. If I did it, I know *you* can, and so much more quickly than I was able to, because you'll have everything I've learned from all my own trial-and-error to help you.

Have you ever felt like you spend a lot of your time and energy looking for your man's good points?

Or trying to explain away why you feel less than satisfied with how he treats you?

Or trying to explain to your friends and family why you've been in a relationship with him for as long as you have without any kind of commitment?

I remember that whenever anyone questioned a relationship I was in — like, "Is he serious?" — I would feel angry with the person asking the question!

I was so sensitive to being "wrong" about a man that I defended him no matter what.

I was "panning for gold."

I couldn't really SEE what was going on — what his intentions toward me were, even what his FEELINGS for me were, that I was always trying to pick up clues.

If you're finding yourself doing this — trying to "get" what every word he says means, trying to read into his actions, being so "understanding" of the challenges of his life, his childhood, his work so that you end up putting your own self "second" to his needs — then this Tool is for you.

How to Stop Panning For His Gold.

STEP 1: Stop assuming he HAS gold!

Yep — what if he looks good "on paper" and perhaps like he stepped out of a magazine ad — but you feel crummy a lot of the time in the relationship?

What if — no matter what you think you know about him, he really is only "what you see is what you get" and he's not showing you very much?

What I want you to do is to take him off his pedestal and look at him NOT from what you HOPE he's like — but what he's shown you so far:

Ask yourself — is he calling me regularly, do I feel good about MYSELF when I'm with him, does he listen to me, do I like his friends and the way he ACTS when he's with his friends?

Ask yourself if the gold you see in him is about HIM — or if he's been "gold" to YOU in your relationship.

STEP 2: Start counting your OWN gold.

This is about paying attention to how much of a prize YOU are, instead of focusing on him.

This is about developing your High Degree of Difficulty and practicing speaking in Feeling Messages to lift your confidence so you can allow yourself to be vulnerable in his presence – all so you can...

STEP 3: Share YOUR gold with him.

This means that instead of focusing on what HE brings to the relationship table – you focus on what YOU have to offer.

And then, instead of always OFFERING what you have to offer, you simply let him SEE your gold, FEEL your gold, and TOUCH you in all your golden glory only when he steps toward you and EARNS your company and a taste of your gold by moving the relationship forward. You are golden, beautiful inside and out, and inspiring.

So – Throw away your "pan" and let your man come to YOU.

15

Be His Truth

$\mathcal{I}$f you've ever held your tongue and not said what you were really feeling because you were afraid of how your man would react, and then things still went downhill — I know how that feels and I can help.

If you've been taught your whole life to hold onto your feelings and pretend to be "cool," "poised" and "together" — like I was — you know how awful that feels inside — and you know, too, how that just doesn't work with men.

We were taught that "telling the truth" scares men away.

When the real "truth" is — NOT telling the truth PUSHES men away!

So – what are we to do?

So much of my work is about stopping pretending, really getting into your real feelings in every moment, and practicing expressing your true feelings in new ways that draw men closer instead of pushing them away...

...and this simple Tool will get the ball rolling for you – TRUTH-TELLING:

1. Get or make a small paper journal you can carry with you (this is great for you to write your feelings in, too, so you can turn them into the Feeling Statements and "Speeches" you're learning how to do in my programs)

2. Wherever you are, whenever you notice you're feeling on edge, or tense around your man – get out your journal and pen and write down the TRUTH -

That could look like:

"I feel so angry when you don't call," or even "I feel actual hatred when you don't call — I want to hit you over the head and shake you." Or,

"I don't feel sexually satisfied in our relationship." Or,

"I wish you made more money," or "I wish you kissed better," or "I don't like the way you dress," or...anything you can think of that's true for you that you never say to your man because you're "nice" and — correctly — don't want to make him wrong.

(This is just paper, remember — you don't have to say any of this to him. Just write it down.)

3. Now, pick a few tiny, not-so-scary truths you've written down, find a private place in your home (or a restaurant bathroom, even), imagine that your man is standing right in front of you, and tell the Truths to him — out loud.

4. Notice how just saying the Truth out loud to your man in your IMAGINATION "Triggers" you in all kinds of ways -

***It might feel scary – you might feel your whole body tightening up.

***You might blank out, shut down, go numb and want to fly away because it feels so scary to say the Truth.

***You might uncover some more anger you're feeling toward him.

***You might feel RELIEVED!

It might feel like a whole lot of tension just dropped off your body, and maybe you'll feel a tiny bit of your sense of HUMOR coming back.

Don't worry about – or even think about – ANY of this.

It's just one more step that will bring your man closer in a deep, emotionally committed way.

The important thing is to FEEL whatever comes up for you.

If you get a powerful insight, or more Truths come up for you — write them down, too!

***Here's an important note: This Tool is only one step in creating "Scripts" for you to speak out loud to a man. This Tool focused on anger, and on feelings you have that feel bad and that you'd consider "negative."

But the truth is, we feel a lot of different things at the same time.

A "Script" might start out with the truth of your warm, loving and respectful feelings, like "I love your sense of humor and how it feels to laugh with you in the kitchen..."

And then you might go into what you want to throw a rock at: "I miss feeling close to you. I miss sex..."

And then you'd let him solve the problem — "What do you think we should do?"

The full guide to how to speak to a man like this is in my ebook, Have The Relationship You Want...and for now, just understanding that you are

ALWAYS going for expressing the TRUTH – the good-feeling truth AND the ugly-feeling truth – and that all those feelings and truths are all present, together, all the time and all at the *same* time for you to choose your words from will help you tremendously.

Practice Telling The Truth – in low-risk, real-life situations and *especially* in the imaginary steps of this Tool. It will make you FEEL stronger, and you'll be on your way to feeling like the amazing "Siren" you already are.

Let me know how Telling The Truth works for you...

16

Be His Pond

*H*ave you ever felt like — if love was a river, it's always flowing AWAY from you?

Like you're somehow the "River of Love," and you're always flowing towards HIM?

And — not only does he NOT appreciate all your beautiful flowing love — a lot of the time he just IGNORES it?

Where's he's like a sponge — soaking up all your love and then wringing himself out somewhere else — not even so much as dripping it back to you?

Like he takes his sponge that's soaked up all

your love and then "wrings" it all over his hobbies, and the TV, and his family, and his work - and leaving NOTHING for you?

I've been there, and I know it feels like torment.

You're always waiting for those drops of love, always looking for the River of Love to change course and start flowing to you from your man.

And not just ONCE, on a special occasion — but ALWAYS — consistently — in a way you can count on.

Well — you can have that.

I know you can, because I was the Queen of flowing my River of Love out to men who barely knew how to even acknowledge me — much less love me at LEAST as much as I loved them.

After a particularly bad breakup, I stayed dateless for over a year.

It's hard to remember what made me pick up my head and notice the men around me who were looking at me and interested in me, but I do remember that those first dates were not dreamy.

If a man was interesting, he wasn't attractive. If a man was attractive, he was mean. If a man was sensitive, he was poor. And if he had money, he was boring.

I couldn't seem to meet a man who even had a few of my basic qualifications. So I stuck to my basic qualification — chemistry.

I remember getting involved with a young man — way younger than myself — where the chemistry was intense, he was smart and fun and interesting, had a good career ahead of him on the horizon — and WAS ABSOLUTELY INCAPABLE OF A SERIOUS RELATIONSHIP.

I mean, it couldn't have been in bigger letters across his forehead.

And still, I dated him, and ONLY him for almost a year. He met my parents, he met my friends, we were "in love."

And a lot of good it did me.

And yet — and here's the really, really important part that helps so many of my clients. What happened in that relationship — the good things as well as the bad, were so VALUABLE in teaching me what I really wanted, what felt good in a relationship, where I needed to compromise some of my "qualifications," where I needed boundaries (a lot of that) and where I was so afraid.

Because, bottom line, the only reason I was in a relationship that couldn't possibly go anywhere was that I was afraid to be in a relationship that WOULD go somewhere.

And the moment I GOT that, I was able to start "dating" men with a completely different attitude.

I was able to learn from every single moment I spent with every man. I was able to learn quickly — and WITHOUT getting so involved I'd experience pain.

I was able to tell the men who were a flowing River of Love from the men who were ponds for receiving all MY love. I was able to identify what was going on with me that kept CHOOSING these "pond" kind of men. I was able to start choosing differently, based more on how I FELT...

And then — like I'd put in a fast-track order for him — my wonderful husband showed up. And you can do it, too.

Here's a letter from Mandy, whose situation is painful, frustrating, and confusing. See if it sounds familiar to you, and we'll work with it together:

"Dear Rori,

My man is great. I shouldn't be complaining. He's steady, reliable — and he ignores me without meaning to.

It's as though if I don't reach out to touch him, kiss him, say hello to him, hug him, call him, ask him how his day was, try to start sex happening - nothing happens.

We can sit on the couch and watch TV together without him even touching me. Or even LOOKING at me. He can just watch the screen like he's in his own world.

If I mention it to him, he's better for a bit - he'll call more or kiss me or hug me more...but it just feels...I don't know...fake...and then it all goes away.

I don't get it. I know he isn't cheating on me.

I know he works hard and he's always thinking about work, and he's nice for the most part, except when he says something cutting or funny/mean...like I did something wrong.

What can I do to get him more interested and...ACTIVE about our relationship? I feel so stuck and confused. And whenever I try to get more affection going — by reaching over to him, often he'll push my hand away.

I know he doesn't mean to hurt me — I just don't get it. Thanks, Mandy"

Here's my answer:

Mandy, if he's a "Pond," that makes you a "River."

It's pretty impossible for two rivers to work together — there would be confusion, butting up against each other — two GIVERS just don't have sexual and emotional chemistry.

But take a river (a Giver) and a pond (a

Receiver) — and it works perfectly.

Your river energy flows into his pond.

Only — if what you REALLY want is to be a POND, as almost ALL of us women do in romantic relationships — then being the river in your relationship will be deeply unsatisfying.

The weird thing is — pond-type men can be very
enticing.

They're often sensitive and fun — and they seem
so unattainable it gives them a kind of "mystery."

And we may have experienced, in our histories, that no one gives to us, no one treats us like we're a lovely, deep, still pond — everyone EXPECTS us to GIVE.

Everyone expects us to be a RIVER.

We are always NEEDED.

And we're taught that this is the way to get a good relationship with a man.

We're taught that if we GIVE, a man

will love us. And it backfires.

For you, Mandy — sometimes a man is just a pond. Just a sponge.

He may have no idea how to be or ACT LIKE a river.

And there's almost no way you can teach him.

(And we try our hardest to teach him, usually by DEMONSTRATING how to Give by doing it ourselves and hoping he'll follow suit — but of course he doesn't and that upsets us even more...)

If you've been following my work, these newsletters and my eBook and programs, you know about Overfunctioning.

You've perhaps (I hope) already stopped initiating conversations and sex and affection.

And still, your man may only step up very little of the time.

So — here's a Tool to increase your POWER in this situation — and that's to: BE A POND.

Okay, so what does that look like — to be a pond?

Well, a pond is a gatherer. Water comes in and stays in the pond, like it's a cup.

A pond is also deep. It has a bottom that's earth, and sometimes the earth gets stirred up and the pond gets cloudy and dark, and sometimes it's still and everything solid falls to the bottom and the pond is clear.

A pond is a RESERVOIR. It HOLDS things.

And, it nurtures ITSELF.

A pond feeds the greenery all around it, and the fish and frogs and one-celled creatures that live in it. A pond supports life.

And if you go to a pond, you can drink, you can find something to eat, you can relax, you can lay down and be yourself.

A pond doesn't jump up when you call or fix dinner when you ask it to.

A pond doesn't start sex, but once you wade in, a pond responds with everything from gentle swirls to powerful waves.

A pond can be small, or a pond can be big – it

can be a LAKE, actually.

So how does that look on the couch when you're watching TV?

That looks like you leaning way back and away from him and putting your feet up on his lap.

That looks like you taking off your shirt and just sitting there topless.

That looks like you having your own snack and not even offering to take care of him.

That looks like you laughing your head off at what you're watching on TV and not even THINKING about HIM or whether or not he's going to touch you.

That looks like, if he's standoffish, saying (during the commercial or when the show's over) "I feel a bit disconnected...is there anything I should know?"

Or..."This feels a bit weird and lonely to me."

Or..."I feel untouched. It doesn't feel good."

Or..."I don't enjoy being invited into the bedroom to join you and you're already lying down...it just feels too...I don't know. I liked it when you grabbed my hair and kissed me passionately that time in the parking lot...I miss that..."

Ponds talk. They speak their feelings. AND a pond does not jump out of the earth.

And...remember this...if a pond does not get watered, by the clouds, or by a stream or river that flows into it — it will dry up.

Do you feel dried up?

That's an awful feeling.

A pond might say "I feel like I'm drying up..."

So — it's not enough to just ACT like a pond and not Overfunction. You have to FEEL like a pond.

You have to not even let your brain get to worrying about what he's doing — because that would be like the pond worrying about how the river is flowing — and ponds don't worry.

Ponds are way too busy supporting all the pond creatures that live inside it — like YOU attend to your body, and your heart, and your hair, and your nails and your feet, and your sensuality and your orgasms, and what's really important to you out in the world, and everything that's related to your PLEASURE.

If he can learn to act like a river — he will.

He'll all of a sudden start flowing to you - because that's what men are programmed to do.

Men we meet and know may have LEARNED to be ponds — but inside their DNA, inside the cells of their bodies, is a HUGE, overpowering desire to be a river and to flow to the woman who can RECEIVE everything he wants to GIVE.

And, if he can't — if he's damaged or broken, or just cannot learn anything new — then you'll know.

And the most amazing thing is — by then — you
won't CARE.

By the time you've settled into the gloriousness of being a pond in a romantic relationship — if he isn't acting like a river, you're going to be bored.

Yes, Mandy — you'll be bored with him. You'll be done.

No pain, no heartache — just "ick...I seem to have lost it for him..."

Try Being a pond. Try imagining yourself not only ACTING like a pond, and leaning back and cutting back on all that you've been doing in the relationship — and try imagining yourself FEELING like a pond.

Soft, in the ground, open, warm, inviting, liquid, constantly changeable and growing — a beautiful combination of dark earth and clear water — a fertile place for love.

And when you sit across from him at dinner, or next to him on the couch in front of the TV — FEEL like a pond.

And let me know what he does.

Be sure to check in with me about your pond-ness — I love the feeling of stillness and POWER it gives me.

About Rori Raye

As a relationship coach, crisis counselor, actress, director, stage producer, mother, author, seminar leader, public speaker and wife of a successful executive coach, I know how challenging it is to balance the masculine energies I use in business and the tasks of daily life with the feminine energies I surrender to in my two-decades-long marriage.

Many years ago, I turned my own conflict-ridden and fading relationship nearly overnight into the vibrant, thrilling, totally satisfying marriage it is now.

My husband is the same man he was during "the awful years," and yet he seems to have changed completely.

I know I've been transformed. From the moment I made my commitment to refuse to try to "manage" my husband and my destiny, my life has been a treasure of peace, fun, love, success and surprises.

Since I turned my own love life around, it's been my mission to help other women rediscover passion and joy in their relationships and marriages. You can interact with me on my blog:

http://blog.HaveTheRelationshipYouWant.com, get my free newsletters at www.HaveTheRelationshipYouWant.com, and work with my ebook and programs 24/7 to get more of the Tools that will help you get the love you want and deserve.

If you visit my blog and make a comment, I'll reply to you right away...and I know you'll get the help you need.

Love, Rori

NOTES

NOTES

NOTES